ISLINGTON

F

Please return this item on or before the last date stamped below or you may be liable to overdue charges. To renew an item call the number below, or access the online catalogue at www.islington.gov.uk/libraries. You will need your library membership number and PIN number.

Islington Libraries

020 7527 6900   www.islington.gov.uk/libraries

whoopie pies

whoopie pies

Fun recipes for filled cookie cakes

Hannah Miles Photography by Steve Painter

RYLAND
PETERS
& SMALL

LONDON NEW YORK

To Ros, a much-missed friend and for her daughters Becca and Aimee.

Photography, design and prop styling
Steve Painter
Senior Commissioning Editor
Julia Charles
Production Toby Marshall
Art Director Leslie Harrington
Publishing Director Alison Starling

Food Stylist Maxine Clark
Index Hilary Bird

First published in the United Kingdom in 2011 by Ryland Peters & Small
20–21 Jockey's Fields
London WC1R 4BW
www.rylandpeters.com

10 9 8 7 6 5 4 3 2 1

Text © Hannah Miles 2011
Design and photographs
© Ryland Peters & Small 2011

Printed in China

ISBN: 978 1 84975 093 6

A CIP record for this book is available from the British Library.

Notes
• All spoon measurements are level unless otherwise specified.
• When using the zest of lemons or limes in a recipe, try to find organic or unwaxed fruits and wash well before using. If you can only find treated fruit, scrub well in warm soapy water and rinse before using.
• Ovens should be preheated to the specified temperatures. All ovens work slightly differently. If using a fan-assisted oven, follow the manufacturer's instructions for adjusting temperatures.
• Although whoopie pies can be made on baking trays, for best results we recommend a whoopie pie cake tin. These are available to order online at www.decuisine.co.uk

Author's Acknowledgements
As ever, a huge thank you to wonderful Ryland Peters & Small for publishing this book, and in particular Julia Charles for knowing that I was a 'whoopie pie kind of gal' and for doing such a kind and patient job editing my recipes. Steve Painter for the wonderful styling and photographs and for going beyond the call of duty to find pink flamingo feathers. Maxine Clark, a kindred spirit, for the beautiful food styling – you transformed my little pies into elegant delights! Heather and Elly at HHB, two very special people who guide me every step of the way. Sacha, Mum, Mike, Dad, Liz, Gareth, Amy, Jane, Geoff, and the Patel family for always being there and for loving me even when I make a mess in the kitchen. My tasters who ate their way through almost 500 pies (may your waistlines forgive me someday); David, Lucy, Kathie, Jess, Miles, Josh, Rosie, Tina, Maren, Alison, Ella, Torin, Peter, Susan, Pauline, Steven, Tena, Pete, Pam, Steve, Ed, Kate and Thomas.

contents

Making whoopie!

The whoopie pie is the ultimate sweet treat. Gone are the days of getting to the bottom of a cupcake with all the frosting already eaten. Whoopie pies are sandwiched together with creamy fillings and can be topped with frosting or a glaze which means that you can enjoy every mouthful. These yummy pies are perfect for coffee breaks, afternoon tea, parties or celebrations – you can even create a whoopie pie wedding cake using the croquembouche recipe on page 56. Whoopie pies are not new and have been an American favourite for decades. The residents of Maine, Pennsylvania and the Amish, all lay claim to the original whoopie, making it difficult to discover the whoopie's true origin, but I am happy to go with the theory that they were given their name by people 'whooping' with delight when they discovered one in their lunch pack. I just love the idea of someone cheering for cake!

Whoopie pies are a cross between a cookie and a cake – softer than a chewy cookie but firmer than a sponge cake. The basic ingredients can generally be found in any kitchen; if you do not have buttermilk in the fridge you can substitute natural yoghurt, soured cream or double cream mixed with the freshly squeezed juice of a lemon, for equally delicious results. Traditionally, whoopie pies are made with vegetable shortening (a solid vegetable fat, such as Trex) but having tested the recipes, I do prefer the flavour that butter gives to the pies. This is entirely a personal preference and you can use the more traditional vegetable shortening in the pie mixture if you prefer. Let your imagination run wild with the colour, flavourings, decorations and sprinkles for these recipes. The whoopie mixture takes colour very well and a small spoon of food colouring paste gives great results.

There are several ways of baking the pies. Whoopie pie tins are available and are similar to bun tins. Each whoopie pie tin makes 12 pie halves and gives the perfect pie dome. If you do not have suitable tins, you can use two large baking trays lined with greaseproof paper or silicone mats. Either make mounds of mixture using an ice cream scoop or shape them with two spoons. For more regular shaped pies (or mini ones) spoon the mixture into a piping bag fitted with a large round nozzle and pipe 6-cm diameter circles directly onto the trays. Whoopie pies are best eaten on the day they are made and recipes containing fresh cream must be refrigerated until you are ready to serve them.

There is something about whoopie pies, perhaps just even their name that just makes people smile. So why not whip up a batch today and spread a little happiness to those you love?

classic pies

classic whoopie pie

These chocolate and marshmallow pies are a true classic. Also known as 'Gobs' or 'Black and Whites', they have a rich chocolate flavour with a creamy marshmallow filling. Sugary sweet and seriously addictive, I promise one bite and you will be hooked! Marshmallow fluff is available in delicatessens and some supermarkets – it is very similar to the creamy white filling you find in the centre of a walnut whip, utterly calorific but quite delicious!

125 g unsalted butter or vegetable shortening, softened

200 g dark soft brown sugar

1 large egg

1 teaspoon vanilla extract

280 g self-raising flour

40 g cocoa powder

1 teaspoon baking powder

½ teaspoon salt

125 ml buttermilk

125 ml soured cream

100 ml hot (not boiling) water

Marshmallow fluff filling

200 g marshmallow fluff

125 g unsalted butter, softened

200 g icing sugar

1 teaspoon vanilla extract

50 ml milk

two 12-hole whoopie pie tins, greased (optional)

a piping bag fitted with a large star nozzle (optional)

Makes 12

Preheat the oven to 180°C (350°F) Gas 4.

To make the pies, cream together the butter and brown sugar in a mixing bowl for 2–3 minutes using an electric hand-held mixer, until light and creamy. Add the egg and vanilla extract and mix again. Sift the flour, cocoa and baking powder into the bowl and add the salt, buttermilk and soured cream. Whisk again until everything is incorporated. Add the hot water and whisk into the mixture.

Put a large spoonful of mixture into each hole in the prepared tins. (Alternatively, use 2 baking trays and follow the instructions given on page 7.) Leave to stand for 10 minutes then bake each tin in the preheated oven for 10–12 minutes. Remove the pies from the oven, let cool slightly then turn out onto a wire rack to cool completely.

To make the filling, whisk together the marshmallow fluff and butter in a mixing bowl using an electric hand-held mixer. Sift in the icing sugar, add the vanilla extract and milk and whisk again for about 3–5 minutes, until light and creamy. Spoon the filling into the prepared piping bag and pipe a generous swirl of filling onto 12 of the whoopie pie halves. (If you do not have a piping bag, spread the filling over the pie halves with a round-bladed knife.) Top with the remaining pie halves and your whoopie pies are ready to enjoy.

red velvet pies

Red velvet cupcakes are an American favourite. The cake is flavoured with cocoa and coloured red, which gives the pies their distinctive look. Sandwiched together with a rich chocolate buttercream and topped with white chocolate, these whoopie pies are a chocoholic's delight!

125 g unsalted butter or vegetable shortening, softened

200 g caster sugar

1 large egg

1 teaspoon vanilla extract

300 g self-raising flour

20 g cocoa powder

1 teaspoon baking powder

½ teaspoon salt

250 ml buttermilk

2 teaspoons red food colouring paste

100 ml hot (not boiling) water

Chocolate buttercream

250 g dark chocolate

160 g unsalted butter

125 g icing sugar

To decorate

300 g white chocolate, melted

cocoa powder, to dust

two 12-hole whoopie pie tins, greased (optional)

a piping bag fitted with a large star nozzle (optional)

Makes 12

Preheat the oven to 180ºC (350ºF) Gas 4.

To make the pies, cream together the butter and caster sugar in a mixing bowl for 2–3 minutes using an electric hand-held mixer, until light and creamy. Add the egg and vanilla extract and mix again. Sift the flour, cocoa and baking powder into the bowl and add the salt, buttermilk and the red food colouring paste. Whisk again until everything is incorporated. Add the hot water and whisk into the mixture.

Put a large spoonful of mixture into each hole in the prepared tins. (Alternatively, use 2 baking trays and follow the instructions given on page 7.) Leave to stand for 10 minutes then bake each tin in the preheated oven for 10–12 minutes. Remove the pies from the oven, let cool slightly then turn out onto a wire rack to cool completely.

To make the chocolate buttercream, break the chocolate into pieces and place in a heatproof bowl set on top of a saucepan of barely simmering water. Take care the bottom of the bowl does not touch the water. Stir until the chocolate has melted. Let the chocolate cool, then whisk together with the butter and icing sugar using an electric whisk. Spoon the buttercream into the prepared piping bag and pipe a generous swirl of buttercream onto 12 of the whoopie pie halves. (If you do not have a piping bag, spread the buttercream over the pie halves with a round-bladed knife.)

To decorate the pie tops, take the remaining pie halves and put them on a sheet of greaseproof paper. Melt the white chocolate following the method given above. Spoon melted chocolate over each one, sufficient to drizzle over the sides. Set aside to cool and set.

Top the buttercream-topped pie halves with the white chocolate-topped pie halves, dust with cocoa powder and your whoopie pies are ready to enjoy.

vanilla dream

Victoria sandwich cake is a classic and much-loved teatime treat. Here, light and fluffy vanilla sponges are filled with a delicate buttercream and raspberry jam to make dainty little pies that are just perfect.

125 g unsalted butter or vegetable shortening, softened

200 g caster sugar

1 large egg

1 teaspoon vanilla extract

320 g self-raising flour

1 teaspoon baking powder

½ teaspoon salt

125 ml buttermilk

125 ml soured cream

100 ml hot (not boiling) water

Vanilla buttercream

90 g unsalted butter, softened

375 g icing sugar, sifted

1 teaspoon vanilla extract

50 ml milk

4 tablespoons raspberry jam

icing sugar, to dust

two 12-hole whoopie pie tins, greased (optional)

a piping bag fitted with a large star nozzle (optional)

Makes 12

Preheat the oven to 180°C (350°F) Gas 4.

To make the pies, cream together the butter and caster sugar in a mixing bowl for 2–3 minutes using an electric hand-held mixer, until light and creamy. Add the egg and vanilla extract and mix again. Sift the flour and baking powder into the bowl and add the salt, buttermilk and soured cream. Whisk again until everything is incorporated. Add the hot water and whisk into the mixture.

Put a large spoonful of mixture into each hole in the prepared tins. (Alternatively, use 2 baking trays and follow the instructions given on page 7.) Leave to stand for 10 minutes then bake the pies in the preheated oven for 10–12 minutes. Remove the pies from the oven, let cool slightly then turn out onto a wire rack to cool completely.

To make the vanilla buttercream, whisk the butter, icing sugar, vanilla extract and milk together in a bowl for 2–3 minutes, until light and creamy. Spoon the buttercream into the prepared piping bag and pipe a swirl of filling onto 12 of the whoopie pie halves. (If you do not have a piping bag, spread the filling over the pie halves with a round-bladed knife.) Put a teaspoon of raspberry jam on top of the buttercream. Top with the remaining pie halves, dust liberally with icing sugar and your whoopie pies are ready to enjoy.

mocha pies

These mocha coffee pies give you the ultimate chocolate, caffeine and sugar hit. It works on so many levels – waking you up and making you feel happy!

125 g unsalted butter or vegetable shortening, softened

100 g dark soft brown sugar

100 g light soft brown sugar

1 large egg

1 teaspoon vanilla extract

280 g self-raising flour

40 g cocoa powder

1 teaspoon baking powder

½ teaspoon salt

250 ml soured cream

1 tablespoon instant coffee, dissolved in 100 ml hot water

100 g dark chocolate chips

Coffee mousse filling

1 tablespoon instant coffee

200 g white chocolate

100 g dark chocolate

300 ml double cream

Coffee icing

1 tablespoon instant coffee

200 g fondant icing sugar powder

To decorate

white chocolate curls

12 chocolate coffee beans

two 12-hole whoopie pie tins, greased (optional)

a piping bag fitted with a large round nozzle (optional)

Makes 12

Preheat the oven to 180°C (350°F) Gas 4.

To make the pies, cream together the butter and brown sugars in a mixing bowl for 2–3 minutes using an electric hand-held mixer, until light and creamy. Add the egg and vanilla extract and mix again. Sift the flour, cocoa and baking powder into the bowl and add the salt and soured cream. Whisk again until everything is incorporated. Add the dissolved coffee and whisk into the mixture. Stir in the chocolate chips.

Put a large spoonful of mixture into each hole in the prepared tins. (Alternatively, use 2 baking trays and follow the instructions given on page 7.) Leave to stand for 10 minutes then bake each tin in the preheated oven for 10–12 minutes. Remove the pies from the oven, let cool slightly then turn out onto a wire rack to cool.

To make the coffee mousse filling, dissolve the coffee in 1 tablespoon hot water. Melt the white and dark chocolates following the method given on page 10 and leave to cool. Whip the double cream to stiff peaks then fold in the melted chocolates and dissolved coffee. Cover and chill in the fridge for 1 hour.

To make the coffee icing, dissolve the coffee in 1 tablespoon hot water and let cool. Add the cooled coffee to the fondant icing sugar and mix with 1–2 tablespoons cold water until you have a smooth icing. Spread the icing over 12 of the pie halves, sprinkle with chocolate curls and finish each one with a chocolate coffee bean in the centre and let the icing set. Spoon the chilled coffee mousse filling into the prepared piping bag and pipe circles of mousse onto the remaining pies halves. (If you do not have a piping bag, spread the filling over the pie halves with a round-bladed knife.) Top with the decorated pie halves and your whoopie pies are ready to enjoy.

pumpkin pies

Warm, buttery, spiced pumpkin pie is a classic autumnal treat. Decorated as cute pumpkins, these whoopie pies make a perfect halloween treat for kids and adults alike!

125 g unsalted butter or vegetable shortening, softened

200 g dark soft brown sugar

1 large egg

140 g tinned pumpkin purée

340 g self-raising flour

2 teaspoons ground cinnamon

1 teaspoon ground mixed spice

1 teaspoon ground ginger

1 teaspoon baking powder

½ teaspoon salt

250 ml natural yoghurt

100 ml hot (not boiling) water

Cream cheese filling

200 g cream cheese

125 g unsalted butter, softened

400 g icing sugar

Orange glacé icing

200 g fondant icing sugar

juice of 1 small orange

orange food colouring

To decorate

3 heaped tablespoons icing sugar

red and green food colouring

2 chocolate sticks

two 12-hole whoopie pie tins, greased (optional)

three piping bags, a small round hole nozzle, a large star nozzle and a leaf nozzle

Makes 12

Preheat the oven to 180ºC (350ºF) Gas 4.

To make the pies, cream together the butter and brown sugar in a mixing bowl for 2–3 minutes using an electric hand-held mixer, until light and creamy. Add the egg and pumpkin purée and mix again. Sift the flour, cinnamon, mixed spice, ginger and baking powder into the bowl and add the salt and yoghurt. Whisk until everything is incorporated. Add the hot water and whisk into the mixture.

Put a large spoonful of mixture into each hole in the prepared tins. (Alternatively, use 2 baking trays and follow the instructions given on page 7.) Leave to stand for 10 minutes then bake each tin in the preheated oven for 10–12 minutes. Remove the pies from the oven, let cool slightly then turn out onto a wire rack to cool completely.

To make the cream cheese filling, whisk together the cream cheese, butter and icing sugar until light and creamy. Remove 4 tablespoons of the mixture, mix in a drop of green food colouring and set aside as this will be used later for decoration. Spoon the remaining filling into a piping bag fitted with the large star nozzle and pipe a generous swirl of filling onto 12 of the pies halves. Set aside.

To make the orange glacé icing, mix together the icing sugar, orange juice and a few drops of orange food colouring until you have smooth glossy icing. Cover the remaining pie halves with the icing using a round-bladed knife and leave to set. When the icing has set, mix 3 tablespoons of icing sugar with 1–2 teaspoons cold water and a few drop of orange and red food colouring to make a thick, darker orange icing. Spoon the icing into a piping bag fitted with a small round hole nozzle and pipe 5 lines from the centre of each pie (to resemble the lines on a pumpkin). Spoon the green cream cheese filling into a clean piping bag fitted with a leaf nozzle and pipe green leaves and a curly stem on top of each pie, as shown. Cut each chocolate stick into 6 pieces and put in the centre to look like stalks.

Top the cream cheese filling-topped pie halves with the decorated pie halves and your whoopie pies are ready to enjoy.

peanut butter and jelly pies

125 g unsalted butter or vegetable shortening, softened

1 tablespoon smooth peanut butter

200 g caster sugar

1 large egg

320 g self-raising flour

1 teaspoon baking powder

½ teaspoon salt

250 ml buttermilk

100 ml hot (not boiling) water

Peanut glaze

1 tablespoon unsalted butter

1 tablespoon smooth peanut butter

150 g icing sugar

50 g salted peanuts, chopped

Filling

70 g unsalted butter, softened

2 tablespoons smooth peanut butter

200 g icing sugar, sifted

3 tablespoons soured cream

3 tablespoons raspberry jam

two 12-hole whoopie pie tins, greased (optional)
a piping bag fitted with a large star nozzle (optional)

Makes 12

Peanut butter and jelly (aka jam!) sandwiches are an all-time American classic – the saltiness of peanuts and sweetness of the jam providing the ultimate sweet and savoury combination.

Preheat the oven to 180ºC (350ºF) Gas 4.

To make the pies, cream together the butter, peanut butter and caster sugar in a mixing bowl for 2–3 minutes using an electric hand-held mixer, until light and creamy. Add the egg and mix again. Sift the flour and baking powder into the bowl and add the salt and buttermilk. Whisk again until everything is incorporated. Add the hot water and whisk into the mixture.

Put a large spoonful of mixture into each hole in the prepared tins. (Alternatively, use 2 baking trays and follow the instructions given on page 7.) Leave to stand for 10 minutes then bake each tin in the preheated oven for 10–12 minutes. Remove the pies from the oven, let cool slightly then turn out onto a wire rack.

To make the peanut glaze, heat the butter, peanut butter, icing sugar and 60 ml cold water in a saucepan set over low heat. Simmer until you have a smooth thick glaze, then spoon this over half of the pie halves. This is best done whilst the pies are still warm on the wire rack and with greaseproof paper underneath to catch any drips. Leave to cool completely.

To make the filling, whisk together the butter, peanut butter, icing sugar and soured cream in a mixing bowl using an electric hand-held mixer, until light and creamy. Spoon the filling into the prepared piping bag and pipe stars of filling in a ring onto the 12 unglazed pie halves – reserving a little to decorate. (If you do not have a piping bag, thickly spread the filling over the pie halves thickly with a round-bladed knife.) Put a spoonful of jam on top of the filling and top with the glazed pie halves. Pipe a star of the reserved filling on top of each one and sprinkle with the chopped peanuts. Your whoopie pies are ready to enjoy.

mini pistachio pies

There are few things more therapeutic than popping pistachios from their shells and eating them – their exotic taste, transporting you to the Middle East, as does this irresistible little pie.

125 g unsalted butter or vegetable shortening, softened

200 g caster sugar

1 large egg

1 teaspoon vanilla extract

320 g self-raising flour

1 teaspoon baking powder

½ teaspoon salt

250 ml natural yoghurt

100 g shelled pistachios, finely chopped

a few drops of green food colouring

100 ml hot (not boiling) water

Meringue filling

2 egg whites

100 g caster sugar

80 g unsalted butter, melted

100 g shelled pistachios, finely ground

To decorate

200 g icing sugar

a few drops of green food colouring

20 g chopped green pistachios

two baking trays, lined with greaseproof paper or silicone mats

a piping bag fitted with a large round nozzle (optional)

Makes 24

Preheat the oven to 180ºC (350ºF) Gas 4.

To make the pies, cream together the butter and caster sugar in a mixing bowl for 2–3 minutes using an electric hand-held mixer, until light and creamy. Add the egg and vanilla extract and mix again. Sift the flour and baking powder into the bowl and add the salt, yoghurt, pistachios and food colouring. Whisk again until everything is incorporated. Add the hot water and whisk into the mixture.

Spoon the mixture into the prepared piping bag and pipe 48 rounds on the prepared trays (about 3-cm diameter) leaving a gap between each one as they will spread during baking. Alternatively, use 2 teaspoons to form small rounds directly onto the trays. Leave to stand for 10 minutes then bake each tray in the preheated oven for 10–12 minutes. Remove the pies from the oven, let cool slightly then transfer to a wire rack to cool.

To make the meringue filling, put the egg whites and sugar in a heatproof bowl set over a saucepan of simmering water, making sure that the bowl does not touch the water. Whisk continuously for 2–3 minutes, until the sugar has dissolved. Remove the bowl from the heat and whisk for 2–3 minutes more, until the meringue forms stiff peaks. Drizzle the melted butter into the meringue whilst still whisking. Fold in the pistachios and chill in the fridge for 3–4 hours.

To decorate, mix the icing sugar and food colouring with 2–3 tablespoons cold water. Spread over 24 of the pie halves and sprinkle with pistachios. Spoon the meringue onto the un-iced halves, top with the iced halves and your whoopie pies are ready to enjoy.

cookies and cream pies

Chocolate and vanilla Oreo cookies dunked in milk are such a treat. Although you can't quite dunk these little pies, they are delicious washed down with a glass of ice-cold milk.

125 g unsalted butter or vegetable shortening, softened

200 g dark soft brown sugar

1 large egg

1 teaspoon vanilla extract

280 g self-raising flour

40 g cocoa powder

1 teaspoon baking powder

½ teaspoon salt

125 ml soured cream

125 ml buttermilk

100 ml hot (not boiling) water

Cookie crumb filling

90 g unsalted butter, softened

375 g icing sugar, sifted

1 teaspoon vanilla extract

60 ml milk

1 tablespoon cocoa powder, sifted

50 g Oreo cookies, or similar

To decorate

150 g white chocolate

12 mini Oreo cookies, or similar

two 12-hole whoopie pie tins, greased (optional)

a piping bag fitted with a large star nozzle (optional)

Makes 12

Preheat the oven to 180°C (350°F) Gas 4.

To make the pies, cream together the butter and brown sugar in a mixing bowl for 2–3 minutes using an electric hand-held mixer, until light and creamy. Add the egg and vanilla extract and mix again. Sift the flour, cocoa and baking powder into the bowl and add the salt, soured cream and buttermilk. Whisk again until everything is incorporated. Add the hot water and whisk into the mixture.

Put a large spoonful of mixture into each hole in the prepared tins. (Alternatively, use 2 baking trays and follow the instructions given on page 7.) Leave to stand for 10 minutes then bake each tin in the preheated oven for 10–12 minutes. Remove the pies from the oven, let cool slightly then turn out onto a wire rack to cool completely.

To decorate, melt the white chocolate following the instructions on page 10, then using a round-bladed knife spread a chocolate semi-circle over 12 of the pie halves. Leave to set.

To make the cookie crumb filling, whisk together the butter, icing sugar, vanilla extract and 50 ml of the milk in a bowl using an electric hand-held mixer, until light and creamy. Remove 2 tablespoons of the buttercream, whisk the cocoa powder into it and set aside to decorate. Blitz the cookies in a food processor to a fine powder. Fold the cookie crumbs and the remaining 10 ml of milk into the remaining buttercream.

Spoon some cookie crumb filling onto the undecorated pie halves and spread thickly with a round-bladed knife. Top each one with a white chocolate-decorated pie half. Put the reserved chocolate buttercream in the prepared piping bag and pipe a star into the centre of each pie. (If you do not have a piping bag, simply use a teaspoon.) Top with a mini Oreo cookie and your whoopie pies are ready to enjoy.

pecan pies

Mouthwatering pecan pie, with its buttery toffee caramel and crunchy nuts, is the inspiration for these, my favourite pies. The filling is made with a pecan praline which has a deliciously sweet and nutty caramel flavour.

125 g unsalted butter or vegetable shortening, softened

200 g dark soft brown sugar

1 large egg

1 tablespoon maple syrup

320 g self-raising flour

1 teaspoon baking powder

½ teaspoon salt

250 ml soured cream

100 ml hot (not boiling) water

Maple glaze

60 g dark soft brown sugar

100 ml maple syrup

2 tablespoons corn syrup

2 tablespoons unsalted butter

Praline cream filling

75 g pecans

100 g caster sugar

300 ml double cream, whipped to stiff peaks

two 12-hole whoopie pie tins, greased (optional)

a piping bag fitted with a large round nozzle (optional)

Makes 12

Preheat the oven to 180ºC (350ºF) Gas 4.

To make the pies, cream together the butter and brown sugar in a mixing bowl for 2–3 minutes using an electric hand-held mixer, until light and creamy. Add the egg and maple syrup and mix again. Sift the flour and baking powder into the bowl and add the salt and soured cream. Whisk again until everything is incorporated. Add the hot water and whisk into the mixture.

Put a large spoonful of mixture into each hole in the prepared tins. (Alternatively, use 2 baking trays and follow the instructions given on page 7.) Leave to stand for 10 minutes then bake each tin in the preheated oven for 10–12 minutes. Remove the pies from the oven, let cool slightly then turn out onto a wire rack.

To make the maple glaze, put the sugar, maple syrup, corn syrup and butter in a saucepan set over gentle heat and warm until the sugar has melted. Drizzle over 12 of the pie halves. This is best done whilst the pies are still warm and on the wire rack, with greaseproof paper underneath to catch any drips. Leave to cool completely.

To make the praline cream filling, sprinkle the pecans over a sheet of greaseproof paper, selecting 12 halves to use for decoration. Warm the caster sugar in a saucepan set over gentle heat, until melted and golden. Do not stir but watch very closely as it will burn easily. As the sugar starts to melt, swirl the pan. When melted, use a spoon to drizzle the caramel over all of the pecans, swirling lacy patterns over the pecans selected for decoration. Once cooled, set the decoration pecans to one side and blitz the remaining ones to a fine dust in a food processor. Fold this praline powder into the whipped cream. Spoon the cream into the prepared piping bag and pipe circles of it onto the unglazed pie halves. (If you do not have a piping bag, spread the filling over the pie halves with a round-bladed knife.) Top with the glazed pie halves and finish each one with a caramel pecan. Your whoopie pies are ready to enjoy.

caramel popcorn pies

I just adore the complete 'kitschness' of these pies, with a caramel glaze and piled high with popcorn. They would be absolutely perfect to serve for a movie night at home.

200 g caster sugar
½ teaspoon sea salt flakes
125 g unsalted butter or vegetable shortening, softened
1 large egg
320 g self-raising flour
1 teaspoon baking powder
250 ml buttermilk

Salted caramel sauce

70 g unsalted butter
50 g dark soft brown sugar
1 tablespoon maple syrup
a pinch of salt
1 tablespoon double cream

Caramel glaze

100 g fondant icing sugar
1 tablespoon salted caramel sauce (see above)
100 g toffee popcorn, to decorate
sugar stars, to sprinkle

Caramel filling

350 g icing sugar
1 tablespoon milk
60 g unsalted butter, softened

two 12-hole whoopie pie tins, greased (optional)
a piping bag fitted with a large star nozzle (optional)

Makes 12

Preheat the oven to 180ºC (350ºF) Gas 4.

To make the pies, gently heat 100 g of the caster sugar in a saucepan, until melted and light golden. Do not stir the sugar whilst it is melting but watch very closely as it will burn easily. As it starts to melt, swirl the pan and when melted, carefully add 100 ml cold water. Continue to heat until the sugar dissolves in the water and then add the salt. Cream together the butter and the remaining caster sugar in a mixing bowl using an electric hand-held mixer, until light and creamy. Add the egg and mix. Sift the flour and baking powder into the bowl and add the buttermilk. Mix until incorporated. Reheat the salted caramel water until hot and whisk into the mixture.

Put a large spoonful of mixture into each hole in the prepared tins. (Alternatively, use 2 baking trays and follow the instructions given on page 7.) Leave to stand for 10 minutes then bake each tin in the preheated oven for 10–12 minutes. Remove the pies from the oven, let cool slightly then turn out onto a wire rack.

To make the salted caramel sauce, put the butter, brown sugar, maple syrup and salt in a saucepan and warm over gentle heat, until the sugar has dissolved. Add the cream to the pan and heat for a few minutes more. Set aside.

To make the caramel glaze, put the icing sugar, 1 tablespoon of the salted caramel sauce and 2 tablespoons cold water in a saucepan. Warm over gentle heat until the sugar has dissolved. Spoon the glaze over 12 of the pie halves, wait a few minutes and spoon over a second coat. This is best done whilst the pies are still warm and on the wire rack, with greaseproof paper underneath to catch any drips. Pile pieces of popcorn on top of the glaze and sprinkle with sugar stars. Leave the glaze to set.

To make the caramel filling, whisk together the icing sugar, milk, butter and remaining salted caramel sauce in a bowl, until light and creamy. Spoon into the prepared piping bag and pipe a swirl onto the unglazed pie halves. (If you do not have a piping bag, spread the filling over the pie halves with a round-bladed knife.) Top with the glazed and popcorn-decorated pie halves and your whoopie pies are ready to enjoy.

fruity pies

chocolate and cherry pies

These indulgent pies are inspired by the classic Black Forest gateaux from Germany – a heady combination of cherries, chocolate and kirsch. For an alcohol-free version omit the kirsch.

80 g dark chocolate

125 g unsalted butter or vegetable shortening, softened

200 g dark soft brown sugar

1 large egg

300 g self-raising flour

20 g cocoa powder

1 teaspoon baking powder

½ teaspoon salt

250 ml natural yoghurt

100 ml hot (not boiling) water

Cherry cream filling

200 g fresh cherries, stoned

2 tablespoons caster sugar

2 tablespoons kirsch (optional)

350 ml double cream, whipped

Chocolate glaze

45 g unsalted butter

90 ml light corn syrup

100 g dark chocolate, broken into pieces

12 fresh cherries with stalks on, to decorate

two 12-hole whoopie pie tins, greased (optional)

Makes 12

Preheat the oven to 180ºC (350ºF) Gas 4.

To make the pies, first melt the dark chocolate following the instructions given on page 10. Cream together the butter and brown sugar in a mixing bowl for 2–3 minutes using an electric hand-held mixer, until light and creamy. Add the egg and mix again. Sift the flour, cocoa and baking powder into the bowl and add the salt, melted chocolate and yoghurt. Whisk again until everything is incorporated. Add the hot water and whisk into the mixture.

Put a large spoonful of mixture into each hole in the prepared tins. (Alternatively, use 2 baking trays and follow the instructions given on page 7.) Leave to stand for 10 minutes then bake each tin for 10–12 minutes in the preheated oven. Remove the pies from the oven, let cool slightly then turn out onto a wire rack.

To make the cherry cream filling, put the cherries in a saucepan with the caster sugar and 100 ml cold water. Simmer over low heat until soft, then remove from the heat. Stir in the kirsch (if using) and set aside to cool. When cooled, fold the cherry compote into the whipped cream, cover and chill in the fridge until needed.

To make the chocolate glaze, heat the butter with the corn syrup, chocolate and 40 ml cold water in a saucepan, until the chocolate and butter have melted and you have a shiny syrup. Spoon the glaze over 12 of the pie halves. This is best done whilst the pies are still warm and on the wire rack and with greaseproof paper underneath to catch any drips. Top each one with a fresh cherry and allow to set for a few minutes.

Spoon some cherry cream filling onto the unglazed pie halves and spread with a round-bladed-knife. Top each one with a glazed and cherry-topped pie half and your whoopie pies are ready to enjoy.

strawberry cream pies

Strawberries and Cream – the epitome of British summertime. Tennis at Wimbledon, picking ripe berries at fruit farms and making homemade strawberry jam. These pies are reminiscent of a classic scone, served with clotted cream and jam.

125 g unsalted butter or vegetable shortening, softened

200 g caster sugar

1 large egg

1 teaspoon vanilla extract

2 teaspoons rose syrup or rose water

320 g self-raising flour

1 teaspoon baking powder

½ teaspoon salt

125 ml buttermilk

125 ml natural yoghurt

100 ml hot (not boiling) water

Strawberry cream filling

400 g fresh strawberries

300 g clotted cream

4 tablespoons strawberry jam

icing sugar, to dust

two 12-hole whoopie pie tins, greased (optional)

Makes 12

Preheat the oven to 180ºC (350ºF) Gas 4.

To make the pies, cream together the butter and caster sugar in a mixing bowl for 2–3 minutes using an electric hand-held mixer, until light and creamy. Add the egg, vanilla extract and rose syrup and mix again. Sift the flour and baking powder into the bowl and add the salt, buttermilk and yoghurt. Whisk again until everything is incorporated. Add the hot water and whisk into the mixture.

Put a large spoonful of mixture into each hole in the prepared tins. (Alternatively, use 2 baking trays and follow the instructions given on page 7.) Leave to stand for 10 minutes then bake each tin in the preheated oven for 10–12 minutes. Remove the pies from the oven, cool slightly then turn out onto a wire rack to cool completely.

To make the strawberry cream filling, remove the hulls and cut the strawberries into slices with a sharp knife. Place a spoonful of clotted cream onto 12 of the pie halves, top each with a teaspoon of strawberry jam and some strawberry slices. Place a remaining pie half on top of each one, dust liberally with icing sugar and your whoopie pies are ready to enjoy.

apple crumble pies

125 g unsalted butter or vegetable shortening, softened

100 g caster sugar

100 g dark soft brown sugar

1 large egg

1 teaspoon ground cinnamon

320 g self-raising flour

1 teaspoon baking powder

½ teaspoon salt

250 ml buttermilk

100 ml hot (not boiling) water

Apple filling

2 large cooking apples

50 g dark soft brown sugar

1 tablespoon unsalted butter

1 teaspoon ground cinnamon

1 tablespoon golden syrup

Crumble topping

50 g self-raising flour

40 g chilled unsalted butter, cubed

30 g caster sugar

Custard filling

200 g white chocolate

200 ml double cream, whipped

200 ml ready-made custard, chilled

two 12-hole whoopie pie tins, greased (optional)

Makes 12

Buttery crumble-topped pies filled with a rich custard and baked apple slices, these pies are quite simply delicious. For an extra special treat, why not serve them for dessert with a jug of warm custard alongside for the ultimate in comfort food.

Preheat the oven to 180°C (350°F) Gas 4.

To make the apple filling, peel, core and thinly slice the apples. Put them in an ovenproof dish and top with the brown sugar, butter, cinnamon, golden syrup and 1 tablespoon cold water. Bake in the preheated oven for 20–25 minutes, until the apple slices are soft but still hold their shape. Set aside to cool. Leave the oven on.

To make the pies, cream together the butter and caster and brown sugars in a mixing bowl for 2–3 minutes using an electric hand-held mixer, until light and creamy. Add the egg and cinnamon and mix again. Sift the flour and baking powder into the bowl and add the salt and buttermilk. Whisk again until everything is incorporated. Add the hot water and whisk into the mixture.

Put a large spoonful of mixture into each hole in the prepared tins. (Alternatively, use 2 baking trays and follow the instructions given on page 7.) Leave to stand for 10 minutes. Meanwhile, make the crumble topping. Put the flour in a bowl and using your fingertips rub in the butter then stir in the caster sugar. Bake the pies in the still-hot oven for 5 minutes, then sprinkle the crumble topping over 12 of the pie halves and bake for a further 5–7 minutes, until golden. Remove the pies from the oven, let cool slightly then turn out onto a wire rack to cool completely.

To make the custard filling, melt the white chocolate following the method given on page 10 and let cool. Gently fold the whipped cream into the custard, along with the melted chocolate. Chill in the fridge for 1–2 hours, then spoon a little custard filling over the pie halves which do not have crumble topping on. Drain the baked apples and put a spoonful on top of the filling. Top with the crumble pie halves and your whoopie pies are ready to enjoy.

lemon sherbet pies

Sherbet lemons are a childhood favourite – sharp lemon sweets with a fizzy treat when you get to the centre. These zingy and zesty pies are just as delicious, with their luscious lemon curd and cream cheese filling and fun sherbet decoration.

125 g unsalted butter or vegetable shortening, softened

200 g caster sugar

1 large egg

finely grated zest of 2 lemons

320 g self-raising flour

1 teaspoon baking powder

½ teaspoon salt

250 ml buttermilk

100 ml hot (not boiling) water

Lemon icing

200 g icing sugar

2–3 tablespoons freshly squeezed lemon juice

Cream cheese filling

200 g cream cheese

2 tablespoons lemon curd

1 tablespoon icing sugar, sifted

To decorate

lemon-flavoured sherbet crystals

12 mini lemon jelly slices

two 12-hole whoopie pie tins, greased (optional)

a piping bag fitted with a large round nozzle (optional)

Makes 12

Preheat the oven to 180ºC (350ºF) Gas 4.

To make the pies, cream together the butter and caster sugar in a mixing bowl for 2–3 minutes using an electric hand-held mixer, until light and creamy. Add the egg and lemon zest and mix again. Sift the flour and baking powder into the bowl and add the salt and buttermilk. Whisk again until everything is incorporated. Add the hot water and whisk into the mixture.

Put a large spoonful of mixture into each hole in the prepared tins. (Alternatively, use 2 baking trays and follow the instructions given on page 7.) Leave to stand for 10 minutes then bake each tin in the preheated oven for 10–12 minutes. Remove the pies from the oven, let cool slightly then turn out onto a wire rack to cool completely.

To make the lemon icing, mix together the icing sugar and lemon juice in a bowl, until it forms a smooth paste. Spread the icing over half of the pie halves and decorate each with a sprinkle of sherbet crystals and a lemon jelly slice.

To make the cream cheese filling, whisk the cream cheese until fluffy and fold in the lemon curd and icing sugar. Put the filling in the prepared piping bag and pipe blobs of filling onto the un-iced pie halves. (If you do not have a piping bag, spread the filling over the pie halves with a round-bladed knife.) Top each with an iced and decorated pie half and your whoopie pies are ready to enjoy.

key lime jelly pies

The tangy citrus jelly filling actually makes these pies wobble – the children who tried them when we tested the recipe loved them and they would be perfect for a kid's party.

125 g unsalted butter or vegetable shortening, softened

200 g caster sugar

1 large egg

finely grated zest of 2 limes

320 g self-raising flour

1 teaspoon baking powder

½ teaspoon salt

250 ml buttermilk

100 ml hot (not boiling) water

Lime jelly filling

4 leaves of gelatine

200 g cream cheese

300 ml soured cream

200 g caster sugar

freshly squeezed juice of 1 orange and 1 lemon

finely grated zest and freshly squeezed juice of 2 limes

a few drops of green food colouring

Lime icing

200 g fondant icing sugar

2–3 tablespoons lime juice

a few drops green food colouring

50 mini lime jelly slices, chopped

two 12-hole whoopie pie tins, greased (optional)

a piping bag fitted with a large star nozzle (optional)

Makes 12

Begin by preparing the lime jelly filling as this will need to set in the fridge for several hours. Soak the gelatine leaves in cold water for about 5 minutes. Put the cream cheese, soured cream and caster sugar in a blender and whizz until mixed. Put the orange, lemon and lime juices and gelatine in a saucepan and heat over very gentle heat until the gelatine has all dissolved. Do not allow it to boil otherwise the gelatine will lose its setting properties. Pour the citrus juice through a sieve into the blender, add the lime zest and a few drops of green food colouring to the blender and mix again. Transfer to a bowl and allow to set in the fridge for about 2–3 hours.

Preheat the oven to 180ºC (350ºF) Gas 4. To make the pies, cream together the butter and caster sugar in a mixing bowl for 2–3 minutes using an electric hand-held mixer, until light and creamy. Add the egg and lime zest and mix again. Sift the flour and baking powder into the bowl and add the salt and buttermilk. Whisk again until everything is incorporated. Add the hot water and whisk into the mixture.

Put a large spoonful of mixture into each hole in the prepared tins. (Alternatively, use 2 baking trays and follow the instructions given on page 7.) Leave to stand for 10 minutes then bake each tin in the preheated oven for 10–12 minutes. Remove the pies from the oven, let cool slightly then turn out onto a wire rack to cool completely.

To make the lime icing, mix together the icing sugar and lime juice, along with the food colouring until it forms a smooth paste. Spread a little over 12 of the pie halves and top with the chopped lime jelly slices. Leave to set. Spoon the lime jelly filling into the prepared piping bag and pipe a swirl of filling onto the un-iced pie halves. (If you do not have a piping bag, spread the filling over the pie halves with a round-bladed knife.) Top each with a decorated pie half and your whoopie pies are ready to enjoy.

Chambord raspberry pies

Raspberries picked straight from the bushes on my mum's allotment are a much anticipated summer treat. Chambord (a raspberry liqueur beautifully presented in a gilded bottle) is delicious with Prosecco or Champagne but I have used it here, in both the glaze and the sumptuous cream filling, to enhance the 'raspberriness' of these luxurious pies.

125 g unsalted butter or vegetable shortening, softened

200 g caster sugar

1 large egg

1 teaspoon vanilla extract

320 g self-raising flour

1 teaspoon baking powder

½ teaspoon salt

250 ml buttermilk

100 ml hot (not boiling) water

Raspberry cream filling

150 ml double cream

250 g mascarpone cheese

2 tablespoons Chambord liqueur

60 g fresh raspberries

Chambord glaze

3 tablespoons icing sugar

2 tablespoons Chambord liqueur

To decorate

12 fresh raspberries

gold leaf (optional)

two 12-hole whoopie pie tins, greased (optional)

a piping bag fitted with a large star nozzle (optional)

Makes 12

Preheat the oven to 180°C (350°F) Gas 4.

To make the pies, cream together the butter and caster sugar in a mixing bowl for 2–3 minutes using an electric hand-held mixer, until light and creamy. Add the egg and vanilla extract and mix again. Sift the flour and baking powder into the bowl and add the salt and buttermilk. Whisk again until everything is incorporated. Add the hot water and whisk into the mixture.

Put a large spoonful of mixture into each hole in the prepared tins. (Alternatively, use 2 baking trays and follow the instructions given on page 7.) Leave to stand for 10 minutes then bake each tin in the preheated oven for 10–12 minutes. Remove the pies from the oven, let cool slightly then turn out onto a wire rack to cool completely.

To make the raspberry cream filling, whip the double cream to stiff peaks. Beat the mascarpone and then whisk it into the cream along with the liqueur and the raspberries. The raspberries will crush as you mix them. Chill in the fridge until you are ready to assemble the pies.

To make the glaze, put the icing sugar, liqueur and 1 tablespoon cold water in a small saucepan and heat until the icing sugar has dissolved. Drizzle the glaze over 12 of the pie halves and top each one with a raspberry. Brush the raspberries with a little of the glaze using a paint brush and press on the gold leaf (if using) with tweezers or the tip of a sharp knife. Spoon the chilled filling into the prepared piping bag and pipe stars of the filling onto the unglazed pie halves. (If you do not have a piping bag, spread the filling over the pie halves with a round-bladed knife.) Top each one with a decorated pie half and your whoopie pies are ready to enjoy.

banoffee pies

Rich caramel-smothered bananas, sandwiched between banana-flavoured pies with fresh cream, make these pies a banoffee lover's delight. Make sure that you use really ripe bananas for a 'true' banana flavour.

1 very ripe banana

freshly squeezed juice of ½ a lemon

125 g unsalted butter or vegetable shortening, softened

200 g caster sugar

1 large egg

340 g self-raising flour

1 teaspoon baking powder

½ teaspoon salt

250 ml soured cream

100 ml hot (not boiling) water

Caramel bananas

2 tablespoons golden syrup

50 g unsalted butter

2 tablespoons dark soft brown sugar

2 tablespoons double cream

2 ripe bananas, sliced

Banana cream

1 very ripe banana, mashed with the freshly squeezed juice of ½ a lemon

300 g clotted cream

12 dried banana chips

two 12-hole whoopie pie tins, greased (optional)

Makes 12

Preheat the oven to 180ºC (350ºF) Gas 4.

To make the pies, mash the banana with the lemon juice in a bowl using a fork. Cream together the butter and caster sugar in a mixing bowl for 2–3 minutes using an electric hand-held mixer, until light and creamy. Add the mashed banana and egg and mix again. Sift the flour and baking powder into the bowl and add the salt and soured cream. Whisk again until everything is incorporated. Add the hot water and whisk into the mixture.

Put a large spoonful of mixture into each hole in the prepared tins. (Alternatively, use 2 baking trays and follow the instructions given on page 7.) Leave to stand for 10 minutes then bake each tin in the preheated oven for 10–12 minutes. Remove the pies from the oven, let cool slightly then turn out onto a wire rack to cool completely.

To make the caramel bananas, gently heat the golden syrup, butter and brown sugar in a saucepan until the sugar has dissolved and you have a smooth caramel sauce. Slowly pour in the double cream and stir until it is incorporated then remove from the heat and allow to cool. When cooled, remove a little sauce and reserve for decoration. Add the banana slices to the saucepan and toss gently using a spoon to ensure the banana slices are well coated.

To make the banana cream, fold the mashed banana into the clotted cream. Spoon some onto 12 of the pie halves, reserving enough to use as a topping. Add a spoonful of caramel bananas and cover with the remaining pie halves. Put a spoonful of the banana cream on top of each pie, add a dried banana chip and a drizzle of the reserved caramel sauce. Your whoopie pies are ready to enjoy.

rose and violet cream pies

I just adore rose and violet creams with their floral fondant fillings, rich dark chocolate shells and crystallized rose and violet petal decorations. I have transferred all these elements to these dainty little pies for the most elegant of teatime treats or the perfect edible gift.

125 g unsalted butter or vegetable shortening, softened

200 g dark soft brown sugar

1 large egg

1 teaspoon vanilla extract

280 g self-raising flour

40 g cocoa powder

1 teaspoon baking powder

½ teaspoon salt

250 ml buttermilk

100 ml hot (not boiling) water

Rose and violet fillings

250 ml double cream

250 g mascarpone cheese

2 tablespoons icing sugar

1 tablespoon rose syrup

1 tablespoon violet syrup

pink and purple food colourings

To decorate

150 g plain chocolate

crystallized rose and violet petals

two baking trays, lined with greaseproof paper or silicone mats

a piping bag fitted with a large round nozzle (optional)

two piping bags, each fitted with a medium round nozzle

24 foil petit four cases

Makes 24

Preheat the oven to 180ºC (350ºF) Gas 4.

To make the pies, cream together the butter and brown sugar in a mixing bowl for 2–3 minutes using an electric hand-held mixer, until light and creamy. Add the egg and vanilla extract and mix again. Sift the flour, cocoa and baking powder into the bowl and add the salt and buttermilk. Whisk again until everything is incorporated. Add the hot water and whisk into the mixture.

Spoon the mixture into the first prepared piping bag and pipe 48 rounds onto the prepared trays (about 3-cm diameter) leaving a gap between each pie as they will spread during baking. (Alternatively, use 2 teaspoons to form small rounds on the trays.) Leave to stand for 10 minutes then bake each tray in the preheated oven for 10–12 minutes. Remove the pies from the oven, let cool slightly then transfer to a wire rack to cool.

To make the fillings, whip the double cream to stiff peaks. In a separate bowl, beat the mascarpone until softened then fold it into the whipped cream along with the icing sugar. Transfer half of the mixture to a separate bowl; add the rose syrup and a few drops of pink food colouring to 1 bowl and the violet syrup and a drop of purple food colouring to the other. Mix both creams well with an electric hand-held mixer.

Spoon the fillings into the remaining prepared piping bags and pipe circles of each flavour onto 12 pie halves, so that you have 24 pie halves covered with cream. Top with the remaining pie halves. To decorate, melt the chocolate following the instructions given on page 10. Spoon a little melted chocolate on each pie, top with a crystallized rose or violet petal, as appropriate to the filling, and allow to set. Put them in petit four cases and your whoopie pies are ready to enjoy.

luxury pies

coconut cloud pies

Eating coconut always transports me to sunnier climes, especially with the addition of coconut rum! Sweetened soft shredded coconut (such as Baker's Angel Flake) works best due to its long strands but desiccated coconut also looks pretty if you are unable to find it.

125 g unsalted butter or vegetable shortening, softened
200 g dark soft brown sugar
1 large egg
320 g self-raising flour
1 teaspoon baking powder
½ teaspoon salt
250 ml soured cream
60 g sweetened shredded coconut
100 ml hot (not boiling) water

Coconut mousse filling

200 g white chocolate
50 ml coconut rum
300 ml double cream
60 g sweetened shredded coconut

To decorate

100 g white chocolate
80 g sweetened shredded coconut

two 12-hole whoopie pie tins, greased (optional)
a piping bag fitted with a large round nozzle (optional)

Makes 12

Begin by preparing the coconut mousse filling as this needs to set in the fridge. Melt the white chocolate following the instructions on page 10 and allow to cool. Add the rum to the double cream and whip to stiff peaks. Fold in the melted chocolate and shredded coconut and chill in the fridge for 1–2 hours, until the mousse has set.

Preheat the oven to 180ºC (350ºF) Gas 4. To make the pies, cream together the butter and brown sugar in a mixing bowl for 2–3 minutes using a hand-held electric mixer, until light and creamy. Add the egg and mix again. Sift the flour and baking powder into the bowl and add the salt, soured cream and coconut. Whisk again until everything is incorporated. Add the hot water and whisk into the mixture.

Put a large spoonful of mixture into each hole in the prepared tins. (Alternatively, use 2 baking trays and follow the instructions given on page 7.) Let stand for 10 minutes then bake each tin in the preheated oven for 10–12 minutes. Remove the pies from the oven, let cool slightly then turn out onto a wire rack to cool completely.

To decorate, melt the white chocolate following the instructions on page 10 and allow to cool. Pour the melted chocolate in a shallow dish and sprinkle the shredded coconut over a flat plate. Roll the sides of each pie half in the chocolate and then in the coconut. Return the pies to the wire rack and let the chocolate set.

Spoon the coconut mousse filling into the prepared piping bag and pipe circles of mousse onto 12 of the decorated pie halves. (If you do not have a piping bag, spread the filling over the pie halves with a round-bladed knife.) Top with the remaining pie halves and your whoopie pies are ready to enjoy.

grasshopper pies

Grasshopper pie was invented in the 1950s and is said to be based on the Grasshopper cocktail with mint, cocoa liqueur and milk. I don't know anyone who doesn't delight in this classic after-dinner flavour combination, refreshing yet indulgent at the same time.

125 g unsalted butter or vegetable shortening, softened

200 g dark soft brown sugar

1 large egg

1 teaspoon peppermint essence

280 g self-raising flour

40 g cocoa powder

1 teaspoon baking powder

½ teaspoon salt

125 ml soured cream

125 ml buttermilk

100 ml hot (not boiling) water

Mint mousse filling

300 g white chocolate

225 ml double cream

1 teaspoon peppermint essence

green food colouring

To decorate

200 g mint-flavoured dark chocolate (not fondant-filled)

green sprinkles (balls or strands)

two 12-hole whoopie pie tins, greased (optional)

a piping bag fitted with a large round nozzle (optional)

Makes 12

Preheat the oven to 180ºC (350ºF) Gas 4.

To make the pies, cream together the butter and brown sugar in a mixing bowl for 2–3 minutes using an electric hand-held mixer, until light and creamy. Add the egg and peppermint essence and mix again. Sift the flour, cocoa and baking powder into the bowl and add the salt, soured cream and buttermilk. Whisk again until everything is incorporated. Add the hot water and whisk into the mixture.

Put a large spoonful of mixture into each hole in the prepared tins. (Alternatively, use 2 baking trays and follow the instructions given on page 7.) Let stand for 10 minutes then bake each tin in the preheated oven for 10–12 minutes. Remove the pies from the oven, let cool slightly then turn out onto a wire rack to cool completely.

To make the mint mousse filling, melt the white chocolate following the instructions given on page 10 and set aside to cool. When the chocolate has cooled but is still runny, whip the double cream to stiff peaks. Pour in the cooled melted chocolate, add the peppermint essence and a few drops of green food colouring and whisk together. Cover and chill the mousse in the fridge for 1 hour.

Meanwhile, melt the mint-flavoured dark chocolate following the instructions given on page 10. Spread it over the top of 12 of the pie halves using a round-bladed knife, scatter over some green sprinkles and leave to set. Spoon the chilled mousse into the prepared piping bag and pipe blobs of the mousse onto the remaining pie halves. (If you do not have a piping bag, spread the filling over the pie halves with a round-bladed knife.) Top with the decorated pie halves and your whoopie pies are ready to enjoy.

almond and amaretto pies

125 g unsalted butter or vegetable shortening, softened

200 g dark soft brown sugar

1 egg

1 teaspoon almond essence

280 g self-raising flour

1 teaspoon baking powder

80 g ground almonds

½ teaspoon salt

250 ml soured cream

1 tablespoon amaretto liqueur

100 ml hot (not boiling) water

Amaretto cream

300 ml double cream

50 ml amaretto liqueur

To decorate

150 g white chocolate

50 g amaretti biscuits, crumbled

two 12-hole whoopie pie tins, greased (optional)

a piping bag fitted with a large star nozzle (optional)

Makes 12

Amaretto is an Italian liqueur made from apricot kernels. These whoopie pies pay homage to this delicious drink with a delicate almond flavour and a crisp amaretti biscuit and white chocolate coating. Serve with a glass of amaretto on ice for a special treat.

Preheat the oven to 180°C (350°F) Gas 4.

To make the pies, cream together the butter and brown sugar in a mixing bowl for 2–3 minutes using an electric hand-held mixer, until light and creamy. Add the egg and almond essence and mix again. Sift the flour and baking powder into the bowl and add the ground almonds, salt, soured cream and amaretto. Whisk again until everything is incorporated. Add the hot water and whisk into the mixture.

Put a large spoonful of mixture into each hole in the prepared tins. (Alternatively, use 2 baking trays and follow the instructions given on page 7.) Let stand for 10 minutes then bake each tin in the preheated oven for 10–12 minutes. Remove the pies from the oven, let cool slightly then turn out onto a wire rack to cool completely.

To decorate the pies, melt the white chocolate following the instructions given on page 10. Sprinkle the amaretti crumbs over a plate and pour the melted chocolate into a shallow dish. Roll the sides of all the pie halves in the chocolate and then roll again in the amaretti crumbs. Return to the wire rack to set. Using a fork, drizzle the tops of 12 of the pie halves with the leftover white chocolate.

To make the amaretto cream filling, put the double cream and amaretto in a mixing bowl and whip to stiff peaks. Spoon into the prepared piping bag and pipe stars of filling onto the 12 pie halves that are not decorated with chocolate on top. (If you do not have a piping bag, spread the filling over the pie halves with a round-bladed knife.) Top with the decorated pie halves and your whoopie pies are ready to enjoy.

gingerbread pies

These pies, inspired by the German soft iced gingerbread Lebkuchen, are a perfect winter treat. If serving as part of your Christmas celebrations, why not let your imagination run wild with the decoration and serve whoopie pies in place of a traditional cake – topped with classic royal icing and decorated with snowy scenes.

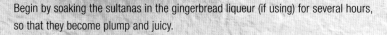

Begin by soaking the sultanas in the gingerbread liqueur (if using) for several hours, so that they become plump and juicy.

Preheat the oven to 180°C (350°F) Gas 4. To make the pies, cream together the butter and brown sugar in a mixing bowl for 2–3 minutes using an electric hand-held mixer, until light and creamy. Add the egg, sultanas and their soaking liquid and mix again. Sift the flour, baking powder, cinnamon, mixed spice and ginger into the bowl and add the salt and soured cream. Whisk again until everything is incorporated. Add the hot water and whisk into the mixture.

Put a large spoonful of mixture into each hole in the prepared tins. (Alternatively, use 2 baking trays and follow the instructions given on page 7.) Leave to stand for 10 minutes then bake each tin in the preheated oven for 10–12. Remove the pies from the oven, let cool slightly then turn out onto a wire rack to cool completely.

To make the icing, whisk the royal icing sugar with 75 ml cold water for about 5 minutes, until the icing is very stiff. Put a tablespoonful of icing on 12 of the pie halves and use a fork to form it into sharp peaks. Arrange a ring of white balls around the outside edge then add a reindeer or Christmas tree to each pie. Leave to set.

To make the ginger cream filling, whisk together the butter, soured cream, icing sugar and gingerbread syrup using an electric hand-held mixer, until light and creamy. Spoon the filling into the prepared piping bag and pipe a swirl onto the un-iced pie halves. (If you don't have a piping bag, spread the filling over the pie halves with a round-bladed knife.) Top with the iced pie halves and your whoopie pies are ready to enjoy.

60 g sultanas

60 ml gingerbread liqueur (optional)

125 g unsalted butter or vegetable shortening, softened

200 g light soft brown sugar

1 large egg

320 g self-raising flour

1 teaspoon baking powder

2 teaspoons ground cinnamon

1 teaspoon ground mixed spice

1 teaspoon ground ginger

250 ml soured cream

½ teaspoon salt

100 ml hot (not boiling) water

Ginger cream filling

125 g unsalted butter

50 ml soured cream

350 g icing sugar

50 ml gingerbread syrup (such as Monin's Pain d'Epices)

Icing and decoration

450 g royal icing sugar

white or silver balls (dragees)

reindeer and/or Christmas trees

two 12-hole whoopie pie tins, greased (optional)

a piping bag fitted with a large star nozzle (optional)

Makes 12

ice cream pies

These pies are a classic chocolate whoopie, just a little bit chillier, and perfect for a barbecue party on a summer's day. You'll need to assemble them at the last minute so that the ice cream doesn't melt. I've used vanilla here but you can substitute any flavour you like – why not try chocolate for a double chocolate treat!

125 g unsalted butter or vegetable shortening, softened

200 g dark soft brown sugar

1 large egg

1 teaspoon vanilla extract

280 g self-raising flour

40 g cocoa powder

1 teaspoon baking powder

½ teaspoon salt

250 ml natural yoghurt

100 ml hot (not boiling) water

Ice cream filling

400 g vanilla ice cream in a block

multicoloured sprinkles, to decorate

two 12-hole whoopie pie tins, greased (optional)

an 8-cm round biscuit cutter

Makes 12

Preheat the oven to 180°C (350°F) Gas 4.

To make the pies, cream together the butter and brown sugar in a mixing bowl for 2–3 minutes using an electric hand-held mixer, until light and creamy. Add the egg and vanilla extract and mix again. Sift the flour, cocoa and baking powder into the bowl and add the salt and yoghurt. Whisk again until everything is incorporated. Add the hot water and whisk into the mixture.

Put a large spoonful of mixture into each hole in the prepared tins. (Alternatively, use 2 baking trays and follow the instructions given on page 7.) Leave to stand for 10 minutes then bake the pies in the preheated oven for 10–12 minutes. Remove the pies from the oven, let cool slightly then turn out onto a wire rack to cool completely.

Shortly before you are ready to serve, remove the ice cream from the freezer and allow to soften slightly. Cut 12 slices each about 2-cm thick and, using the biscuit cutter, stamp out a round from each slice. Sandwich an ice cream round between 2 cooled pie halves. Working quickly, put the sprinkles on a flat plate and roll each pie in them so that the ice cream is coated. Serve your whoopie pies immediately with napkins to catch any ice cream drips.

party
pies

valentine heart pies

As a special treat for loved ones on Valentine's Day, why not make these pretty pies. With strawberries, cherries, cranberries, white chocolate chips and a pink chocolate glaze, what could be a more romantic way of showing you care?

125 g unsalted butter or vegetable shortening, softened

200 g caster sugar

1 large egg

1 teaspoon vanilla extract

320 g self-raising flour

1 teaspoon baking powder

½ teaspoon salt

250 ml natural yoghurt

50 g dried cranberries

50 g dried soured cherries

50 g white chocolate chips

100 ml hot (not boiling) water

Strawberry cream filling

200 g fresh strawberries

2 tablespoons caster sugar

freshly squeezed juice of ½ a lemon

300 ml double cream

Pink chocolate glaze

150 g white chocolate

60 ml corn syrup

20 g unsalted butter

a few drops of pink food colouring

assorted heart-shaped sprinkles, to decorate

two 6-hole heart-shaped cupcake tins, greased (optional)

a piping bag fitted with a large star nozzle (optional)

Makes 12

Preheat the oven to 180ºC (350ºF) Gas 4.

To make the pies, cream together the butter and caster sugar in a mixing bowl for 2–3 minutes using an electric hand-held mixer, until light and creamy. Add the egg and vanilla extract and mix again. Sift the flour and baking powder into the bowl and add the salt, yoghurt, cranberries, cherries and chocolate chips. Whisk again until everything is incorporated. Add the hot water and whisk into the mixture.

Put a large spoonful of mixture into each hole in the prepared tins. (Alternatively, use 2 baking trays and follow the instructions given on page 7, but piping the mixture into heart shapes.) Leave to stand for 10 minutes then bake each tin in the preheated oven for 10–12 minutes. Remove the pies from the oven, let cool slightly then turn out onto a wire rack to cool completely.

To make the filling, put the strawberries, caster sugar and lemon juice in a small saucepan and add 60 ml cold water. Simmer over low heat, until the strawberries are very soft. Purée until smooth in a blender and set aside to cool. Whip the double cream to stiff peaks then fold in the cooled strawberry purée. Chill until required.

To make the pink chocolate glaze, put the white chocolate, corn syrup, butter and 30 ml cold water in a bowl and set over a pan of simmering water. Heat until the chocolate has melted and you have a smooth syrup. Add the pink food colouring. Spoon the glaze over 12 of the pie halves, wait 5 minutes then spoon over a second coat. This is best done whilst the pies are still on the wire rack and with greaseproof paper underneath to catch any drips. Sprinkle over the sugar hearts and leave to set.

Spoon the strawberry cream filling into the prepared piping bag and pipe a generous swirl of cream onto the unglazed pie halves. (If you don't have a piping bag, spread the filling over the pie halves with a round-bladed knife.) Top each one with a glazed pie half. Your whoopie pies are now ready to enjoy.

whoopie croquembouche

This is the ultimate celebration of the wonderful whoopie pie, a giant stack of pies inspired by the French profiterole tower known as a croquembouche. A perfect centrepiece for a party or even a wedding, as you can make the pies any colour you wish to fit in with your colour scheme.

500 g unsalted butter or vegetable shortening, softened

800 g caster sugar

4 large eggs

4 teaspoon vanilla extract

1.28 kg self-raising flour

4 teaspoons baking powder

2 teaspoons salt

500 ml buttermilk

500 ml soured cream

400 ml hot (not boiling) water

red, orange, yellow, green, blue and purple food colourings

Buttercream filling

375 g unsalted butter, softened

1.5 kg icing sugar, sifted

190 ml milk

2 teaspoons vanilla extract

eight 12-hole whoopie pie tins, greased (or you can cook in batches if you do not have enough tins or baking trays)

a piping bag fitted with a large star nozzle (optional)

a cone made with thin cardboard, 25-cm diameter and 25-cm tall

9-m thin ribbon in various colours

a long metal skewer with a ring

Makes 1 croquembouche (47 individual pies)

Preheat the oven to 180°C (350°F) Gas 4.

To make the pies, cream together the butter and sugar in a very large mixing bowl for 2–3 minutes using an electric hand-held mixer, until light and creamy. (Because of the large quantities required, you may prefer to make the mixture up in 2 batches.) Add the eggs and vanilla extract and mix again. Sift the flour and baking powder into the bowl and add the salt, buttermilk and soured cream. Whisk again until everything is incorporated. Add the hot water and whisk into the mixture.

Divide the mixture into 6 separate bowls ready for colouring, allowing a heaped tablespoon of mixture for each whoopie pie half. Add food colouring to make 10 red, 12 orange, 14 yellow, 16 green, 20 blue and 22 purple pie halves. Place a large spoonful of mixture into each hole in the prepared tins. (Alternatively, use 4 baking trays and follow the instructions given on page 7.) Leave to stand for 10 minutes then bake each tin in the preheated oven for 10–12 minutes. Remove the pies from the oven, let cool slightly then turn out on a wire rack to cool completely.

To make the buttercream filling, whisk together the butter, icing sugar, milk and vanilla extract for 2–3 minutes, until light and creamy. Spoon into the prepared piping bag and pipe a swirl between each pair of pies. (If you do not have a piping bag, spread the filling over the pie halves with a knife.) Reserve a little buttercream for assembly.

To assemble the tower, begin by cutting the top off of the prepared cardboard cone to remove the point. Place the cone on a cake stand or similar and fix in place with the reserved buttercream. Put the purple pies around the base of the cone and the repeat with the remaining colours until your tower is assembled. Tie the ribbons to the ring of the skewer and push it through the pie at the top of the tower. Lower the skewer into the top open end of the cone to secure the top pie. Arrange the ribbons around the tower and your whoopie pie croquembouche is now ready to dazzle!

giant birthday whoopie pie

What could be more fun than celebrating a birthday with this oversized whoopie pie? The recipe has a rich chocolate glaze, classic marshmallow filling and fresh strawberries and you can finish it with candles and any decorations that you like.

125 g unsalted butter or vegetable shortening, softened

200 g dark soft brown sugar

1 large egg

1 teaspoon vanilla extract

280 g self-raising flour

40 g cocoa powder

1 teaspoon baking powder

½ teaspoon salt

250 ml soured cream

100 ml hot (not boiling) water

Marshmallow fluff filling

200 g marshmallow fluff (see page 9)

125 g unsalted butter, softened

200 g icing sugar

1 teaspoon vanilla extract

50 ml milk

150 g fresh strawberries, hulled and halved

Chocolate icing

150 g icing sugar

30 g cocoa powder

white and dark chocolate curls, edible rice paper (wafer) flowers, sprinkles and candles, to decorate

2 large baking trays, greased and lined with greaseproof paper

a piping bag fitted with a large star nozzle (optional)

Preheat the oven to 180ºC (350ºF) Gas 4.

To make the pies, cream together the butter and brown sugar in a mixing bowl for 2–3 minutes using an electric hand-held mixer, until light and creamy. Add the egg and vanilla extract and mix again. Sift the flour, cocoa and baking powder into the bowl and add the salt and soured cream. Whisk again until everything is incorporated. Add the hot water and whisk into the mixture.

Divide the mixture between the prepared baking trays and spread each out into a 23-cm circle. Leave to stand for 10 minutes then bake each tray in the preheated oven for 12–15 minutes. Remove the pies from the oven and let cool completely on the trays.

To make the filling, whisk together the marshmallow fluff and butter using an electric hand-held mixer. Sift in the icing sugar, add the vanilla extract and milk and whisk again for 3–5 minutes, until light and creamy. Spoon the filling into the prepared piping bag. Put one of the pie halves on a cake stand and pipe a row of stars around the outside edge, alternating with the strawberries. Pipe the remaining filling in a continuous swirl, working towards the centre of the pie base. Top with the remaining strawberries and put the other pie half on top. (If you don't have a piping bag, spread the filling over the pie half with a round-bladed knife and put the strawberries on top.)

To make the chocolate icing, mix the icing sugar, cocoa and 30 ml cold water to a smooth paste. Spread over the top of the pie cake and decorate as shown or as desired. Allow the icing to set and your giant whoopie pie is now ready to enjoy.

Serves 10-12

flamingo pies

125 g unsalted butter or vegetable shortening, softened

200 g caster sugar

1 large egg

1 teaspoon pink food colouring

1 teaspoon vanilla extract

320 g self-raising flour

1 teaspoon baking powder

½ teaspoon salt

250 ml buttermilk

100 ml hot (not boiling) water

Pink cream filling

1 teaspoon pink food colouring

300 ml double cream

Icing and decoration

200 g icing sugar

pink and orange food colouring

1 teaspoon vanilla extract

60 g sweetened soft shredded coconut (such as Baker's Angel Flakes)

edible glitter and sparkles

two 12-hole whoopie pie tins, greased (optional)

Makes 12

These are the pinkest of pies. I served these at an 'Alice in Wonderland' themed tea party in honour of the flamingo croquet match played between Alice and the Queen of Hearts. Serve decorated with pink feathers for the ultimate flamingo fandango!

Preheat the oven to 180°C (350°F) Gas 4.

To make the pies, cream together the butter and caster sugar in a mixing bowl for 2–3 minutes using an electric hand-held mixer, until light and creamy. Add the egg, pink food colouring and vanilla extract and mix again. Sift the flour and baking powder into the bowl and add the salt and buttermilk. Whisk again until everything is incorporated. Add the hot water and whisk into the mixture.

Put a large spoonful of mixture into each hole in the prepared tins. (Alternatively, use 2 baking trays and follow the instructions given on page 7.) Leave to stand for 10 minutes then bake each tin in the preheated oven for 10–12 minutes. Remove the pies from the oven, let cool slightly then turn out onto a wire rack to cool completely.

To make the icing, mix the icing sugar, 2–3 teaspoons cold water, a few drops of pink food colouring and the vanilla extract to a smooth paste. Divide the shredded coconut between 2 bowls; add pink food colouring to 1 and orange food colouring to the other and mix until coloured. Spoon the pink icing over 12 of the pie halves. This is best done whilst the pies are still on the wire rack, with greaseproof paper underneath to catch any drips. Sprinkle with the pink and orange shredded coconut and dust with glitter and sparkles. Allow the icing to set.

To make the pink cream filling, add a few drops of pink food colouring to the double cream and whip to stiff peaks. Put a spoonful of filling on top of the 12 un-iced pie halves and spread with a round-bladed knife. Top with the iced pie halves and your whoopie pies are ready to enjoy.

oyster pies

125 g unsalted butter or vegetable shortening, softened

200 g caster sugar

1 egg

1 teaspoon vanilla extract

320 g self-raising flour

1 teaspoon baking powder

½ teaspoon salt

125 ml natural yoghurt

125 ml soured cream

100 ml hot (not boiling) water

Filling and decoration

7 tablespoons icing sugar

3–4 tablespoons marshmallow fluff

white sprinkles (ideally tiny balls)

400 ml double cream

10 sugar pearls

300 g digestive biscuits (optional)

two 6-hole shell-shaped baking tins, greased

a piping bag fitted with a small round nozzle

a piping bag fitted with a large star nozzle

Makes 12

Served on biscuit crumb 'sand', these amusing pies are perfect for any beach-themed party. You will need a baking tin with shell-shaped moulds, as it's not possible to create the shape by any other means. Bake in two batches if you can only find one tin.

Preheat the oven to 180°C (350°F) Gas 4.

To make the pies, cream together the butter and caster sugar in a mixing bowl for 2–3 minutes using an electric hand-held mixer, until light and creamy. Add the egg and vanilla extract and mix again. Sift the flour and baking powder into the bowl and add the salt, yoghurt and soured cream. Whisk again until everything is incorporated. Add the hot water and whisk into the mixture.

Put a large spoonful of mixture into each hole in the prepared tins. Leave to stand for 10 minutes then bake the pies in the preheated oven for 10–12 minutes. Remove the pies from the oven, let cool slightly and then turn out onto cool on a wire rack to cool completely.

To decorate, mix the icing sugar and 2–3 teaspoons cold water to a thick smooth paste. Spoon the icing into the piping bag fitted with a small round nozzle and pipe fine lines on top of 12 of the pie halves, as shown. Use a round-bladed knife to spread a little marshmallow fluff around the front edges of the iced pie halves and roll them in the sprinkles to decorate. Set aside.

To make the 'seafoam' filling, whip the cream to stiff peaks then spoon into it the piping bag fitted with a large star nozzle. Pipe lines of cream onto the undecorated pie halves, as shown, and add a sugar pearl. Top each one with a decorated pie half.

Crush the biscuits, if using, in a food processor or put them in a polythene bag and bash with a rolling pin to make fine crumbs. Sprinkle over a serving plate or tray and place your oyster pies on top of the 'sand'. Your whoopie pies are now ready to enjoy.

index